Embracing Serenity - The Art of Slowing Down and Discovering Life's Beauty

Anelly Aya

Table of Contents

Introduction: Navigating the Chaos 2
Chapter 1: The Importance of Slowing Down 4
Chapter 2: Finding Stillness in a Fast-Paced World 6
Chapter 3: Overcoming Decision Paralysis 8
Chapter 4: The Crossroads of Life: Choosing Your Path 10
Chapter 5: Embracing Uncertainty with Courage 12
Chapter 6: Rediscovering Joy in Everyday Moments 14
Chapter 7: Cultivating Mindfulness in Daily Life 16
Chapter 8: The Power of Intentional Living 18
Chapter 9: Letting Go of Productivity Obsession 20
Chapter 10: Unraveling the Myth of Busyness 22
Chapter 11: The Beauty of Leisure and Hobbies 24
Chapter 12: Baking Therapy: Finding Peace in the Kitchen 26
Chapter 13: Immersing Yourself in the World of Fiction 28
Chapter 14: The Healing Power of Nature 30
Chapter 15: Exploring the Wonders of the Great Outdoors 32
Chapter 16: Capturing Moments of Beauty Through Photography 34
Chapter 17: Embracing Creativity as a Form of Self-Expression 36
Chapter 18: Building Meaningful Connections in a Digital Age 38
Chapter 19: Nurturing Relationships Through Quality Time 40
Chapter 20: The Art of Simple Pleasures 42
Chapter 21: Letting Nature Guide Your Journey 44
Chapter 22: Embracing Imperfection and Finding Peace 46

Chapter 23: Embracing Imperfection and Finding Peace 48
Chapter 24: Living Authentically: Honoring Your True Self 50
Chapter 25: Cultivating Gratitude and Appreciation 52
Chapter 26: The Journey of Self-Discovery 54
Chapter: Conclusion - Embracing Serenity in a Chaotic World 56

Introduction: Navigating the Chaos

In the hustle and bustle of modern life, it's easy to feel overwhelmed by the constant noise and chaos that surrounds us. From the moment we wake up to the sound of our alarms to the endless stream of notifications on our phones, it often feels like we're being pulled in a million different directions at once. In this chapter, we'll explore the concept of navigating the chaos, finding moments of stillness amidst the storm, and embarking on a journey towards serenity and inner peace.

The world we live in today is characterized by its fast pace and relentless demands. We're constantly bombarded with information, expectations, and obligations, leaving little time for rest and reflection. As a result, many of us find ourselves caught in a perpetual cycle of stress and anxiety, struggling to keep up with the never-ending demands of modern life.

But amidst the chaos, there lies an opportunity – an opportunity to pause, to breathe, and to reclaim a sense of calm amidst the storm. Navigating the chaos doesn't mean avoiding it altogether; rather, it's about finding ways to navigate through it with grace and resilience. It's about learning to ride the waves of life's challenges without losing sight of our inner peace and well-being.

One of the first steps in navigating the chaos is learning to cultivate mindfulness – the practice of being present in the moment and fully engaged in our experiences. Mindfulness allows us to step back from the chaos of our thoughts and emotions, giving us the space we need to observe them with clarity and compassion. By practicing mindfulness, we can develop greater self-awareness and emotional resilience, enabling us to navigate life's challenges with greater ease and grace.

Another essential aspect of navigating the chaos is learning to set boundaries and prioritize our time and energy. In a world where we're constantly bombarded with demands and distractions, it's easy to spread ourselves too thin and lose sight of what truly matters. By setting clear boundaries and learning to say no to things that don't align with our values and priorities, we can create space for the things that truly nourish and sustain us.

But perhaps the most important aspect of navigating the chaos is learning to embrace impermanence and uncertainty. Life is inherently unpredictable, and no matter how much we try to control it, there will always be times when things don't go according to plan. Learning to embrace the ebb and flow of life's ups and downs, and to trust in the wisdom of the universe, is essential for navigating the chaos with grace and resilience.

As we embark on this journey of navigating the chaos, it's important to remember that we're not alone. We're all in this together, navigating the same stormy seas of life, and supporting each other along the way. By reaching out to others for support and connection, and by offering our own support and compassion in return, we can navigate the chaos with greater ease and grace.

Summary: In this chapter, we've explored the concept of navigating the chaos – finding moments of stillness amidst the storm and embarking on a journey towards serenity and inner peace. We've discussed the importance of cultivating mindfulness, setting boundaries, and embracing impermanence and uncertainty. As we continue on this journey, let us remember that we're not alone, and that together, we can navigate the chaos with grace and resilience.

Chapter 1: The Importance of Slowing Down

In a world where speed and efficiency are often prized above all else, the concept of slowing down may seem counterintuitive. However, in this chapter, we will explore the profound importance of slowing down in our lives, and how it can lead to greater peace, happiness, and fulfillment.

At its core, the importance of slowing down lies in its ability to counteract the frenetic pace of modern life and provide us with much-needed respite from the constant hustle and bustle. When we slow down, we give ourselves the opportunity to reconnect with our inner selves, to savor the present moment, and to appreciate the beauty and richness of life that often pass us by in our rush to keep up with the demands of the world around us.

Slowing down also allows us to cultivate a deeper sense of presence and mindfulness in our daily lives. When we're constantly rushing from one task to the next, our minds are often scattered and fragmented, making it difficult to focus on the task at hand or to fully engage with the people and experiences around us. By slowing down and paying attention to the present moment, we can cultivate greater clarity, focus, and awareness, leading to a more meaningful and fulfilling life.

Moreover, slowing down can have profound benefits for our physical and mental well-being. The constant stress and pressure of modern life can take a toll on our health, leading to a host of physical and emotional ailments such as anxiety, depression, and burnout. Slowing down allows us to break free from the cycle of stress and overwhelm, giving our bodies and minds the opportunity to rest, recharge, and rejuvenate.

In addition, slowing down can help us cultivate a greater sense of gratitude and appreciation for the simple joys and pleasures of life. When we're constantly rushing from one thing to the next, it's easy to take the beauty and richness of life for granted. By slowing down and taking the time to savor life's small moments – a beautiful sunset, a heartfelt conversation with a loved one, or the simple pleasure of a home-cooked meal – we can cultivate a deeper sense of gratitude and appreciation for the blessings that surround us.

Furthermore, slowing down can lead to greater creativity and innovation in our lives. When we're constantly busy and distracted, our minds are often too cluttered to allow for the emergence of new ideas and insights. By slowing down and giving ourselves the space to breathe and reflect, we create the conditions for creativity to flourish. Whether it's through quiet contemplation, leisurely walks in nature, or simply taking the time to daydream, slowing down can help us tap into our innate creativity and unlock new possibilities in our lives.

Finally, slowing down can lead to greater overall life satisfaction and fulfillment. In our fast-paced society, it's easy to equate success with busyness and productivity, leading many of us to constantly strive for more, without ever taking the time to pause and ask ourselves what truly brings us joy and fulfillment. By slowing down and tuning into our inner selves, we can gain greater clarity about our values, priorities, and goals, allowing us to live more authentically and in alignment with our deepest desires and aspirations.

Summary: In this chapter, we've explored the profound importance of slowing down in our lives. We've discussed how slowing down can counteract the frenetic pace of modern life, cultivate greater presence and mindfulness, promote physical and mental well-being, foster gratitude and appreciation, stimulate creativity and innovation, and lead to greater overall life satisfaction and fulfillment. As we continue on our journey, let us remember the importance of slowing down and embracing the beauty of the present moment.

Chapter 2: Finding Stillness in a Fast-Paced World

In today's fast-paced world, finding moments of stillness and tranquility can seem like an elusive goal. With the constant demands of work, family, and social obligations, it's easy to feel overwhelmed and frazzled, constantly running from one task to the next without ever pausing to catch our breath. However, in this chapter, we will explore the importance of finding stillness in the midst of life's chaos, and how doing so can lead to greater peace, clarity, and well-being.

At its core, finding stillness is about creating moments of quiet and calm amidst the noise and busyness of everyday life. It's about carving out sacred space for ourselves to simply be, without the pressure to constantly do and achieve. In a world that glorifies busyness and productivity, finding stillness can feel like a radical act of self-care and self-preservation.

One of the most powerful ways to find stillness in a fast-paced world is through the practice of mindfulness meditation. Mindfulness meditation involves bringing our full attention to the present moment, without judgment or attachment to the thoughts and feelings that arise. By focusing on our breath, bodily sensations, or the sounds and sights around us, we can anchor ourselves in the present moment and cultivate a sense of inner calm and peace.

Another way to find stillness is by immersing ourselves in nature. Spending time in natural settings, such as parks, forests, or gardens, can have a profound calming effect on the mind and body. The sights, sounds, and smells of nature can help us slow down, relax, and reconnect with the rhythms of the natural world. Whether it's going for a leisurely walk in the woods, sitting by a tranquil lake, or simply gazing up at the stars on a clear night, nature has a way of soothing our souls and reminding us of the beauty and wonder of life.

Additionally, finding stillness can involve engaging in activities that bring us joy and relaxation, such as reading, listening to music, or practicing yoga. These activities allow us to step out of the whirlwind of daily life and into a space of calm and serenity. By immersing ourselves in activities that nourish our souls and replenish our spirits, we can recharge our batteries and approach life with renewed energy and vitality.

Furthermore, finding stillness is about cultivating an inner sanctuary within ourselves – a place of refuge where we can retreat to whenever life becomes overwhelming or chaotic. This inner sanctuary can take many forms, whether it's a physical space in our home where we can meditate or practice mindfulness, or simply a mental space that we can access whenever we need to center ourselves and find peace amidst the storm.

In conclusion, finding stillness in a fast-paced world is essential for our physical, mental, and emotional well-being. By carving out moments of quiet and calm amidst the chaos of daily life, we can cultivate greater peace, clarity, and resilience in the face of life's challenges. Whether it's through mindfulness meditation, spending time in nature, engaging in relaxing activities, or cultivating an inner sanctuary within ourselves, finding stillness is a powerful tool for navigating the complexities of modern life with grace and ease.

Summary: In this chapter, we've explored the importance of finding stillness in a fast-paced world. We've discussed how practices such as mindfulness meditation, spending time in nature, engaging in relaxing activities, and cultivating an inner sanctuary can help us carve out moments of quiet and calm amidst the chaos of daily life. As we continue on our journey, let us remember the importance of finding stillness and embracing the peace and clarity that it brings.

Chapter 3: Overcoming Decision Paralysis

In the intricate tapestry of life, we often find ourselves at crossroads, faced with the daunting task of making decisions that can shape our future. However, for many of us, the fear of making the wrong choice can lead to a state of paralysis, where we feel unable to move forward or take action. In this chapter, we will delve into the phenomenon known as decision paralysis, explore its underlying causes, and discover strategies for overcoming it.

Decision paralysis, also known as analysis paralysis or choice overload, refers to the state of being unable to make a decision due to an overwhelming array of options or fear of making the wrong choice. It often stems from a fear of failure or the consequences of making a mistake, leading to feelings of anxiety, indecision, and self-doubt.

One of the primary causes of decision paralysis is the abundance of choices available to us in today's society. From simple decisions like what to wear or what to eat, to more complex decisions like which career path to pursue or where to live, we are bombarded with an endless array of options at every turn. This abundance of choice can lead to decision fatigue, making it difficult to make even the simplest of decisions.

Another common cause of decision paralysis is perfectionism – the belief that we must make the perfect choice or achieve the perfect outcome in order to be successful or worthy. This relentless pursuit of perfection can paralyze us with fear, preventing us from taking action or making decisions for fear of falling short of our own impossibly high standards.

Furthermore, decision paralysis can be exacerbated by external pressures and expectations from society, family, or peers. We may feel pressured to conform to societal norms or expectations, leading us to second-guess ourselves or hesitate to make decisions that go against the grain.

So how can we overcome decision paralysis and move forward with confidence and clarity? One strategy is to simplify the decision-making process by breaking it down into smaller, more manageable steps. Instead of trying to weigh all the pros and cons at once, focus on identifying the most important criteria or factors that will influence your decision, and prioritize them accordingly.

Another effective strategy is to set clear goals and priorities before making a decision. By clarifying what you hope to achieve or what matters most to you in the long run, you can narrow down your options and make decisions that align with your values and aspirations.

Additionally, it can be helpful to seek support and guidance from trusted friends, family members, or mentors when faced with difficult decisions. Talking through your options with someone you trust can provide valuable insights, perspective, and reassurance, helping you gain clarity and confidence in your decision-making process.

Furthermore, practicing self-compassion and embracing the possibility of failure can help alleviate the fear and anxiety associated with decision paralysis. Remember that making mistakes is a natural part of the learning process, and that failure is not a reflection of your worth or competence as a person.

In conclusion, decision paralysis is a common obstacle that many of us face on our journey through life. However, by understanding its underlying causes and implementing strategies to overcome it, we can break free from the grip of indecision and move forward with confidence and clarity. By simplifying the decision-making process, setting clear goals and priorities, seeking support and guidance, and practicing self-compassion, we can navigate life's many choices with grace and ease.

Summary: In this chapter, we've explored the phenomenon of decision paralysis and its underlying causes, such as choice overload, perfectionism, and external pressures. We've also discussed strategies for overcoming decision paralysis, including simplifying the decision-making process, setting clear goals and priorities, seeking support and guidance, and practicing self-compassion. As we continue on our journey, let us remember that indecision is not a permanent state, and that with patience, perseverance, and self-awareness, we can break free from the paralysis of indecision and move forward with confidence and clarity.

Chapter 4: The Crossroads of Life: Choosing Your Path

Life is a journey filled with twists and turns, highs and lows, and countless opportunities for growth and self-discovery. At various points along this journey, we inevitably find ourselves standing at the crossroads, faced with the daunting task of choosing which path to take. In this chapter, we will explore the significance of these pivotal moments, the factors that influence our decision-making process, and the importance of choosing a path that aligns with our values, passions, and aspirations.

Standing at the crossroads of life, we are confronted with a multitude of options and possibilities, each leading in a different direction and holding the potential to shape our future in profound ways. Whether it's deciding which career path to pursue, which relationships to invest in, or which dreams to chase, the choices we make at these pivotal moments can have far-reaching consequences that reverberate throughout our lives.

One of the key factors that influence our decision-making process at the crossroads of life is our values and beliefs. Our values serve as guiding principles that inform our decisions and shape our priorities, helping us discern which paths align with our deepest desires and aspirations. When faced with difficult decisions, it's essential to reflect on our values and consider how each option aligns with our core beliefs and principles.

Another important consideration when choosing our path is our passions and interests. What excites us? What ignites our curiosity and drives us to pursue our dreams with passion and enthusiasm? By tapping into our passions and interests, we can find clarity and direction in our decision-making process, guiding us towards paths that resonate with our authentic selves.

Furthermore, it's crucial to consider the long-term implications of our choices when standing at the crossroads of life. While some paths may offer immediate gratification or temporary relief, others may lead to greater fulfillment, growth, and self-actualization in the long run. By taking a holistic view of our options and considering their potential long-term consequences, we can make decisions that align with our broader goals and aspirations.

However, navigating the crossroads of life can be daunting, and it's natural to feel overwhelmed or uncertain about which path to take. In moments of indecision, it can be helpful to seek guidance and support from trusted friends, family members, or mentors who can offer valuable insights, perspective, and encouragement. Additionally, practicing self-reflection, journaling, or meditation can help clarify our thoughts and feelings, allowing us to tune into our intuition and inner wisdom.

Ultimately, the key to choosing our path lies in embracing our authenticity and trusting ourselves to make decisions that honor our values, passions, and aspirations. By listening to our inner voice, following our heart, and staying true to ourselves, we can navigate the crossroads of life with confidence, courage, and clarity.

Summary: In this chapter, we've explored the significance of the crossroads of life, where we are faced with pivotal decisions that shape our future. We've discussed the factors that influence our decision-making process, including our values, passions, and long-term goals. We've also highlighted the importance of seeking guidance and support, practicing self-reflection, and trusting our intuition when navigating these pivotal moments. As we continue on our journey, let us embrace the opportunities for growth and self-discovery that arise at the crossroads of life, and choose paths that lead us closer to our dreams and aspirations.

Chapter 5: Embracing Uncertainty with Courage

Life is inherently uncertain, filled with unpredictability and ambiguity at every turn. Yet, it is our ability to embrace this uncertainty with courage and resilience that enables us to navigate the ever-changing landscape of existence. In this chapter, we delve into the art of embracing uncertainty, exploring how to confront fear, cultivate resilience, and find peace amidst life's inevitable unpredictability.

Uncertainty is a natural part of the human experience, yet it often evokes feelings of fear, anxiety, and discomfort. We fear the unknown, the unpredictable nature of the future, and the possibility of failure or disappointment. However, it is through embracing this uncertainty with courage that we can transform fear into opportunity and growth.

At its core, courage is not the absence of fear, but rather the willingness to confront fear and take action despite it. It is the ability to step into the unknown, to embrace vulnerability, and to trust in our own resilience and strength. When faced with uncertainty, we have a choice – to shrink back in fear or to lean into discomfort with courage and conviction.

One of the key components of embracing uncertainty with courage is cultivating resilience – the ability to bounce back from adversity, to adapt to change, and to find strength in the face of challenges. Resilience is not about avoiding difficult situations or denying our emotions; rather, it is about facing adversity head-on, learning from setbacks, and emerging stronger and more resilient as a result.

Moreover, embracing uncertainty with courage requires us to adopt a mindset of openness and curiosity. Instead of viewing uncertainty as a threat, we can see it as an opportunity for growth, exploration, and discovery. By approaching uncertainty with a sense of curiosity and wonder, we can expand our horizons, learn new things, and embrace the richness and diversity of life's experiences.

Practicing mindfulness and presence is another powerful tool for embracing uncertainty with courage. By cultivating awareness of the present moment and learning to let go of worries about the future, we can find peace and clarity amidst life's uncertainties. Mindfulness allows us to ground ourselves in the here and now, to savor life's simple pleasures, and to find joy and contentment in the present moment.

Furthermore, connecting with others and building a supportive community can provide a source of strength and resilience when facing uncertainty. By sharing our fears, hopes, and struggles with trusted friends, family members, or colleagues, we can find comfort, encouragement, and solidarity in our shared humanity.

In summary, embracing uncertainty with courage is a transformative practice that allows us to navigate life's unpredictable twists and turns with grace and resilience. By confronting fear, cultivating resilience, adopting a mindset of openness and curiosity, practicing mindfulness and presence, and building supportive connections, we can embrace uncertainty as an opportunity for growth, learning, and self-discovery. As we continue on our journey, let us lean into uncertainty with courage and conviction, trusting in our own strength and resilience to carry us through life's inevitable challenges and uncertainties.

Summary: In this chapter, we explored the art of embracing uncertainty with courage. We discussed the importance of confronting fear, cultivating resilience, adopting a mindset of openness and curiosity, practicing mindfulness and presence, and building supportive connections. By embracing uncertainty with courage, we can navigate life's unpredictable twists and turns with grace and resilience, finding strength and opportunity in the face of adversity. As we continue on our journey, let us lean into uncertainty with courage and conviction, trusting in our own resilience and strength to carry us through life's inevitable challenges and uncertainties.

Chapter 6: Rediscovering Joy in Everyday Moments

In the hustle and bustle of modern life, it's easy to overlook the beauty and joy that surrounds us in the ordinary moments of our daily existence. Yet, it is often in these seemingly mundane moments that true happiness and fulfillment can be found. In this chapter, we explore the importance of rediscovering joy in everyday moments, and how doing so can profoundly enhance our quality of life.

The pace of modern life is relentless, with endless to-do lists, commitments, and obligations vying for our attention. In the midst of this chaos, it's easy to become disconnected from the present moment, lost in a whirlwind of thoughts about the past or worries about the future. However, by learning to slow down and cultivate mindfulness, we can begin to appreciate the richness and beauty of the present moment.

Mindfulness is the practice of paying attention to the present moment with openness, curiosity, and acceptance. It involves bringing awareness to our thoughts, feelings, sensations, and surroundings without judgment or attachment. Through mindfulness, we can learn to savor the simple pleasures of life, such as the warmth of the sun on our skin, the sound of birdsong in the morning, or the taste of a delicious meal shared with loved ones.

Moreover, cultivating gratitude is another powerful way to rediscover joy in everyday moments. By taking time each day to reflect on the things we are grateful for, we can shift our focus from what is lacking in our lives to the abundance that surrounds us. Gratitude helps us to cultivate a sense of awe and appreciation for the beauty and wonder of life, even in the most ordinary of moments.

Connecting with nature is also an effective way to rediscover joy in everyday moments. Spending time outdoors, whether it's going for a walk in the park, hiking in the mountains, or simply sitting in a garden, can help to ground us in the present moment and foster a sense of connection with the natural world. Nature has a way of reminding us of the simple joys of life – the beauty of a sunset, the majesty of a towering tree, or the tranquility of a babbling brook.

Furthermore, engaging in activities that bring us joy and fulfillment is essential for rediscovering joy in everyday moments. Whether it's pursuing a hobby, spending time with loved ones, or engaging in creative expression, finding activities that nourish our souls and bring us pleasure is vital for our overall well-being. These activities remind us of the inherent joy and wonder of being alive and help to infuse our lives with meaning and purpose.

In summary, rediscovering joy in everyday moments is a transformative practice that can profoundly enhance our quality of life. By cultivating mindfulness, practicing gratitude, connecting with nature, and engaging in activities that bring us joy and fulfillment, we can learn to savor the simple pleasures of life and find happiness and contentment in the present moment. As we continue on our journey, let us embrace the beauty and wonder of the ordinary moments that make life truly meaningful.

Summary: In this chapter, we explored the importance of rediscovering joy in everyday moments. We discussed the role of mindfulness, gratitude, nature, and joyful activities in cultivating a deeper appreciation for the present moment. By learning to savor the simple pleasures of life and finding happiness and contentment in the ordinary moments, we can profoundly enhance our quality of life. As we continue on our journey, let us embrace the beauty and wonder of everyday life, finding joy and fulfillment in the here and now.

Chapter 7: Cultivating Mindfulness in Daily Life

In today's fast-paced world, it's easy to get swept up in the chaos of daily life and lose touch with the present moment. However, by cultivating mindfulness, we can learn to bring our awareness back to the here and now, fostering a greater sense of peace, clarity, and well-being. In this chapter, we explore the practice of mindfulness and how it can be integrated into our daily lives.

Mindfulness is the practice of paying attention to the present moment with openness, curiosity, and acceptance. It involves bringing awareness to our thoughts, feelings, sensations, and surroundings without judgment or attachment. Through mindfulness, we can learn to observe our experiences with greater clarity and compassion, allowing us to respond to life's challenges with grace and resilience.

One of the most accessible ways to cultivate mindfulness in daily life is through mindfulness meditation. Meditation involves sitting quietly and paying attention to the sensations of the breath as it moves in and out of the body. By focusing on the breath, we can anchor our awareness in the present moment and cultivate a sense of inner calm and stillness.

Another effective way to cultivate mindfulness is through mindful walking. Mindful walking involves bringing awareness to each step as we walk, noticing the sensations of the feet touching the ground, the movement of the body, and the sights and sounds of our surroundings. Walking mindfully can help to ground us in the present moment and foster a sense of connection with the world around us.

Furthermore, integrating mindfulness into everyday activities such as eating, drinking, and even washing dishes can help to bring greater awareness and presence to our daily lives. By paying attention to the sensations, tastes, and textures of our experiences, we can cultivate a deeper appreciation for the simple pleasures of life and nourish our bodies and minds.

Practicing mindfulness also involves learning to observe our thoughts and emotions with detachment and equanimity. Rather than getting caught up in the stories and dramas of our minds, we can learn to step back and observe our thoughts and feelings with curiosity and compassion. This allows us to respond to life's challenges with greater clarity and wisdom, rather than reacting impulsively out of habit or fear.

Moreover, cultivating mindfulness can help to reduce stress, anxiety, and depression, and improve overall mental health and well-being. By learning to be present with our experiences, we can develop a greater sense of inner peace and resilience in the face of life's ups and downs. Mindfulness also fosters a deeper connection with ourselves and others, allowing us to cultivate more meaningful and fulfilling relationships.

In summary, cultivating mindfulness in daily life is a transformative practice that can enhance our quality of life in profound ways. By learning to bring our awareness back to the present moment, we can cultivate a greater sense of peace, clarity, and well-being. As we continue on our journey, let us embrace the practice of mindfulness with openness, curiosity, and compassion, allowing it to enrich every aspect of our lives.

Summary: In this chapter, we explored the practice of cultivating mindfulness in daily life. We discussed the role of mindfulness meditation, mindful walking, and integrating mindfulness into everyday activities in fostering a greater sense of presence and well-being. By learning to observe our thoughts and emotions with detachment and equanimity, we can respond to life's challenges with greater clarity and wisdom. Cultivating mindfulness can also help to reduce stress, anxiety, and depression, and improve overall mental health and well-being. As we continue on our journey, let us embrace the practice of mindfulness with openness, curiosity, and compassion, allowing it to enrich every aspect of our lives.

Chapter 8: The Power of Intentional Living

In a world filled with distractions and noise, intentional living offers a path to greater clarity, purpose, and fulfillment. It's about making conscious choices that align with our values, goals, and priorities, rather than simply reacting to external stimuli. In this chapter, we delve into the transformative power of intentional living and how it can positively impact every aspect of our lives.

At its core, intentional living is about living with purpose and mindfulness. It involves clarifying what truly matters to us and making deliberate choices that support our vision for the future. By setting clear intentions and aligning our actions with our values, we can create a life that is meaningful, fulfilling, and authentic.

One of the key principles of intentional living is mindfulness, or the practice of being present and aware in each moment. Mindfulness allows us to tune into our inner wisdom and intuition, helping us make decisions that are in alignment with our highest selves. By cultivating mindfulness, we can break free from the autopilot mode of living and take control of our lives with greater intentionality.

Intentional living also involves setting goals and priorities that reflect our values and aspirations. By identifying what we truly want to achieve in life, we can focus our time, energy, and resources on the things that matter most to us. This sense of clarity and purpose can drive us forward, even in the face of obstacles and challenges.

Furthermore, intentional living encourages us to simplify our lives and let go of anything that no longer serves us. By decluttering our physical space, simplifying our schedules, and minimizing distractions, we can create more room for the things that bring us joy and fulfillment. This minimalist approach to life can lead to greater clarity, peace of mind, and freedom.

Another important aspect of intentional living is cultivating gratitude and appreciation for the present moment. By pausing to acknowledge the blessings and abundance in our lives, we can cultivate a sense of contentment and fulfillment that transcends material possessions and external achievements. Gratitude helps us stay grounded in the present moment and find joy in the simple pleasures of life.

Moreover, intentional living encourages us to foster deeper connections with ourselves and others. By investing time and energy in nurturing meaningful relationships, we can experience greater fulfillment and belonging. Intentional living also involves setting boundaries and saying no to commitments that drain our energy or detract from our well-being, allowing us to prioritize self-care and cultivate healthy, supportive relationships.

In summary, intentional living is a transformative practice that empowers us to live with greater purpose, clarity, and fulfillment. By making conscious choices that align with our values and priorities, we can create a life that is meaningful, authentic, and deeply satisfying. As we continue on our journey, let us embrace the power of intentional living with open hearts and open minds, knowing that each choice we make has the potential to shape our destiny.

Summary: In this chapter, we explored the concept of intentional living and its transformative power to create a life of purpose and fulfillment. Intentional living involves making conscious choices that align with our values, goals, and priorities, and cultivating mindfulness and gratitude in every moment. By simplifying our lives, setting clear goals, and nurturing meaningful relationships, we can experience greater clarity, peace, and joy. As we continue on our journey, let us embrace the power of intentional living with open hearts and open minds, knowing that each choice we make has the potential to shape our destiny.

Chapter 9: Letting Go of Productivity Obsession

In today's fast-paced world, productivity has become synonymous with success. We're constantly bombarded with messages that encourage us to hustle harder, work longer hours, and optimize every aspect of our lives for maximum efficiency. However, in our relentless pursuit of productivity, we often overlook the importance of rest, leisure, and simply being present in the moment. In this chapter, we explore the detrimental effects of productivity obsession and the benefits of letting go and embracing a more balanced approach to life.

Productivity obsession stems from the belief that our worth is tied to our output—that we must constantly be achieving, producing, and accomplishing in order to feel valuable and worthy. This mindset can lead to chronic stress, burnout, and a sense of never feeling "good enough." Moreover, it can erode our sense of self-worth and identity, as we become increasingly defined by our productivity levels.

The truth is, productivity alone does not equate to happiness or fulfillment. While achieving our goals and making progress is important, it's equally crucial to prioritize our well-being, relationships, and overall quality of life. Constantly pushing ourselves to the brink of exhaustion in the name of productivity only serves to diminish our enjoyment of life and detract from our overall happiness.

Letting go of productivity obsession involves challenging the deeply ingrained belief that our value is contingent upon our productivity levels. It requires us to redefine success on our own terms and prioritize self-care, rest, and leisure as essential components of a fulfilling life. This means giving ourselves permission to slow down, take breaks, and engage in activities that bring us joy and rejuvenation, even if they don't directly contribute to our productivity.

One of the biggest challenges in letting go of productivity obsession is overcoming the fear of falling behind or failing to meet expectations. We live in a society that glorifies busyness and achievement, often at the expense of our mental and physical well-being. However, true success lies in finding a balance between productivity and self-care, and recognizing that our worth is inherent and not dependent on external accomplishments.

Embracing a more balanced approach to life involves setting boundaries, saying no to unnecessary commitments, and prioritizing our health and happiness above all else. It means allowing ourselves to rest without guilt, and giving ourselves permission to pursue activities purely for the sake of enjoyment, rather than productivity. By letting go of productivity obsession, we can experience greater peace, fulfillment, and overall well-being.

In summary, letting go of productivity obsession is essential for cultivating a life of balance, happiness, and fulfillment. It involves challenging societal norms and redefining success on our own terms. By prioritizing self-care, rest, and leisure, we can break free from the cycle of chronic stress and burnout, and embrace a more holistic approach to life. As we continue on our journey, let us remember that our worth is not determined by our productivity levels, but by the depth of our connections, the richness of our experiences, and the love in our hearts.

Summary: In this chapter, we explored the detrimental effects of productivity obsession and the importance of letting go and embracing a more balanced approach to life. Productivity obsession can lead to chronic stress, burnout, and a diminished sense of self-worth. Letting go of productivity obsession involves challenging societal norms and redefining success on our own terms. By prioritizing self-care, rest, and leisure, we can break free from the cycle of chronic stress and burnout, and experience greater peace and fulfillment. As we continue on our journey, let us remember that our worth is not determined by our productivity levels, but by the richness of our experiences and the love in our hearts.

Chapter 10: Unraveling the Myth of Busyness

In modern society, busyness has become a badge of honor—a symbol of productivity, success, and importance. We wear our packed schedules like a badge of honor, proudly boasting about how busy we are and how little time we have for leisure or relaxation. However, beneath the surface of this glorification of busyness lies a dangerous myth—one that perpetuates stress, burnout, and a constant feeling of being overwhelmed. In this chapter, we delve into the myth of busyness and explore the detrimental effects it has on our well-being and overall quality of life.

The myth of busyness is rooted in the belief that being busy equates to being productive and successful. We live in a culture that values productivity above all else, often at the expense of our mental and physical health. From the moment we wake up to the moment we go to bed, we're bombarded with demands and distractions that pull us in a million different directions, leaving us feeling exhausted and depleted.

The reality is that busyness does not necessarily equate to productivity. In fact, constantly being busy can hinder our ability to focus, prioritize, and accomplish our goals effectively. It can also lead to chronic stress, anxiety, and burnout, as we struggle to keep up with the relentless pace of modern life.

Moreover, the glorification of busyness perpetuates a culture of comparison and competition, where we feel pressure to constantly outdo ourselves and others in terms of productivity and achievement. This constant need to prove ourselves and measure up to unrealistic standards only serves to fuel our feelings of inadequacy and insecurity.

To unravel the myth of busyness, we must challenge the belief that our worth is tied to our level of productivity. We must learn to prioritize our well-being and set boundaries around our time and energy, saying no to unnecessary commitments and carving out space for rest and relaxation. We must also cultivate a mindset of mindfulness and presence, learning to slow down and savor the moments of peace and quiet amidst the chaos of daily life.

Breaking free from the myth of busyness requires us to reevaluate our values and redefine success on our own terms. It means recognizing that true success is not measured by how much we accomplish or how busy we are, but by the quality of our relationships, the depth of our experiences, and the level of fulfillment and happiness we experience in our lives.

In summary, the myth of busyness perpetuates stress, burnout, and a constant feeling of being overwhelmed. To unravel this myth, we must challenge the belief that our worth is tied to our level of productivity and learn to prioritize our well-being and presence. By setting boundaries, cultivating mindfulness, and redefining success on our own terms, we can break free from the cycle of busyness and experience greater peace, fulfillment, and joy in our lives.

Summary: In this chapter, we explored the detrimental effects of the myth of busyness on our well-being and overall quality of life. Busyness is rooted in the belief that being busy equates to being productive and successful, but in reality, it often leads to stress, burnout, and a constant feeling of being overwhelmed. To unravel the myth of busyness, we must challenge the belief that our worth is tied to our level of productivity and learn to prioritize our well-being and presence. By setting boundaries, cultivating mindfulness, and redefining success on our own terms, we can break free from the cycle of busyness and experience greater peace, fulfillment, and joy in our lives.

Chapter 11: The Beauty of Leisure and Hobbies

In today's fast-paced world, leisure and hobbies are often overlooked in favor of productivity and achievement. However, embracing leisure activities and hobbies is essential for our overall well-being and happiness. In this chapter, we explore the beauty of leisure and hobbies and their profound impact on our physical, mental, and emotional health.

Leisure activities and hobbies provide us with much-needed downtime and relaxation, allowing us to recharge our batteries and alleviate stress. Engaging in activities that we enjoy can help to reduce cortisol levels, lower blood pressure, and promote feelings of calm and relaxation. Whether it's reading a book, gardening, or painting, carving out time for leisure activities can significantly improve our overall quality of life.

Furthermore, hobbies offer us a sense of purpose and fulfillment, allowing us to express our creativity and pursue our passions. Engaging in activities that we love can boost our self-esteem and confidence, as we develop new skills and accomplish meaningful goals. Whether it's playing a musical instrument, cooking, or woodworking, hobbies provide us with a sense of accomplishment and satisfaction that transcends the demands of daily life.

Leisure activities and hobbies also foster social connection and community, allowing us to bond with others who share similar interests. Whether it's joining a book club, participating in a sports team, or attending a cooking class, hobbies provide us with opportunities to meet new people and forge meaningful connections. These social interactions are essential for our mental and emotional well-being, helping to combat feelings of loneliness and isolation.

Moreover, leisure activities and hobbies encourage us to live in the present moment, fostering mindfulness and appreciation for the beauty of life. Engaging in activities that bring us joy allows us to escape from the stresses of everyday life and immerse ourselves fully in the present moment. Whether it's hiking in nature, practicing yoga, or photography, hobbies encourage us to slow down and savor the simple pleasures of life.

In summary, leisure activities and hobbies play a vital role in our overall well-being and happiness. They provide us with much-needed downtime and relaxation, foster creativity and self-expression, promote social connection and community, and encourage mindfulness and appreciation for the beauty of life. By embracing leisure activities and hobbies, we can cultivate a greater sense of fulfillment, joy, and balance in our lives.

Summary: In this chapter, we explored the beauty of leisure activities and hobbies and their profound impact on our physical, mental, and emotional well-being. Leisure activities provide us with much-needed downtime and relaxation, while hobbies offer us a sense of purpose and fulfillment. Additionally, leisure activities and hobbies foster social connection and community, encourage mindfulness, and appreciation for the beauty of life. By embracing leisure activities and hobbies, we can cultivate a greater sense of fulfillment, joy, and balance in our lives.

Chapter 12: Baking Therapy: Finding Peace in the Kitchen

In the hustle and bustle of modern life, finding moments of tranquility can be challenging. However, one activity that offers a sanctuary of calmness and joy is baking. In this chapter, we delve into the therapeutic benefits of baking and how it can provide a source of solace and relaxation in our lives.

Baking is more than just a culinary endeavor; it's a form of therapy that allows us to express creativity, alleviate stress, and nourish both body and soul. The process of measuring ingredients, mixing batter, and watching as dough rises in the oven can be incredibly soothing and meditative. As we knead dough or decorate cookies, we enter a state of flow where our minds are fully absorbed in the task at hand, free from worries or distractions.

Furthermore, baking engages all of our senses, providing a multi-sensory experience that can evoke feelings of comfort and nostalgia. The smell of freshly baked bread or cookies wafting through the kitchen can transport us back to cherished memories of home and family. The sight of a beautifully decorated cake or pastry can delight our eyes and fill us with a sense of accomplishment. The taste of a warm, gooey brownie can tantalize our taste buds and bring us moments of pure bliss.

Baking also allows us to connect with others and share the fruits of our labor with loved ones. Whether we're baking a batch of cookies for a friend or preparing a homemade pie for a family gathering, the act of sharing homemade treats fosters bonds and creates lasting memories. Baking can be a social activity, bringing people together to bake, decorate, and enjoy delicious creations.

Moreover, baking has therapeutic benefits for our mental health and well-being. The repetitive actions involved in baking can be calming and soothing, providing an outlet for stress and anxiety. Baking also allows us to express our creativity and channel our emotions into something tangible and delicious. The sense of accomplishment that comes from baking a beautiful cake or perfecting a new recipe can boost our self-esteem and confidence.

In summary, baking therapy offers a unique opportunity to find peace and serenity in the kitchen. Through the process of baking, we can engage our senses, express creativity, connect with others, and nourish our bodies and souls. Whether we're kneading dough, frosting cupcakes, or pulling a warm loaf of bread from the oven, baking allows us to slow down, savor the moment, and find joy in the simple pleasures of life.

Summary: In this chapter, we explored the therapeutic benefits of baking and how it can provide a source of solace and relaxation in our lives. Baking engages all of our senses and offers a multi-sensory experience that can evoke feelings of comfort and nostalgia. Baking also allows us to connect with others, share homemade treats, and create lasting memories. Moreover, baking has therapeutic benefits for our mental health and well-being, providing an outlet for stress and anxiety, boosting self-esteem and confidence, and fostering creativity and expression. Overall, baking therapy offers a unique opportunity to find peace and serenity in the kitchen and enjoy the simple pleasures of life.

Chapter 13: Immersing Yourself in the World of Fiction

In a fast-paced world filled with distractions, finding moments of peace and escape can be challenging. However, one avenue that offers a retreat from the chaos of everyday life is the world of fiction. In this chapter, we explore the transformative power of literature and how immersing ourselves in fiction can provide a sanctuary for the mind and soul.

Fiction has the remarkable ability to transport us to different times, places, and realities, allowing us to step outside of our own lives and experience the world through the eyes of others. Whether it's a thrilling adventure, a heart-wrenching romance, or a thought-provoking mystery, fiction offers a diverse array of stories and genres to suit every taste and preference.

When we dive into a work of fiction, we enter a realm of imagination where anything is possible. We become engrossed in the lives of fictional characters, following their journeys, experiencing their triumphs and tribulations, and empathizing with their struggles and emotions. Through the power of storytelling, we gain insights into the human condition and develop a deeper understanding of ourselves and others.

Moreover, reading fiction stimulates our minds and ignites our imaginations, providing mental stimulation and cognitive benefits. Studies have shown that reading fiction can improve empathy, increase emotional intelligence, and enhance critical thinking skills. By engaging with complex narratives and diverse perspectives, we broaden our horizons and cultivate a more nuanced understanding of the world around us.

Furthermore, immersing ourselves in fiction offers a form of escapism, allowing us to temporarily escape the stresses and pressures of reality. In the pages of a novel, we can find solace, relaxation, and a sense of comfort. Fiction provides a refuge from the noise and chaos of the outside world, offering a quiet space for reflection, introspection, and self-discovery.

In today's digital age, where screens and technology dominate our lives, the simple act of reading a book can feel like a revolutionary act of resistance. By unplugging from devices and immersing ourselves in the written word, we reclaim our time and attention, reconnect with our humanity, and rediscover the joy of slow, mindful reading.

In summary, immersing yourself in the world of fiction offers a myriad of benefits for the mind, body, and soul. Fiction provides an escape from reality, a source of inspiration and insight, and a means of mental stimulation and cognitive growth. Whether you're curling up with a classic novel, getting lost in a fantasy epic, or exploring the pages of a contemporary bestseller, fiction has the power to transport you to new worlds, broaden your horizons, and enrich your life in countless ways.

Summary: In this chapter, we explored the transformative power of fiction and how immersing ourselves in the world of literature can provide a sanctuary for the mind and soul. Fiction allows us to escape from reality, gain insights into the human condition, and stimulate our minds. By unplugging from screens and immersing ourselves in the written word, we reclaim our time and attention, reconnect with our humanity, and rediscover the joy of slow, mindful reading. Overall, fiction offers a myriad of benefits for personal growth, introspection, and self-discovery, making it an invaluable tool for navigating the complexities of modern life.

Chapter 14: The Healing Power of Nature

In a world filled with constant noise and distractions, finding moments of peace and solace can seem like an elusive dream. However, amidst the chaos of modern life, there exists a sanctuary of serenity waiting to be discovered – the healing embrace of nature. In this chapter, we delve into the profound impact that nature has on our physical, mental, and emotional well-being, and explore how reconnecting with the natural world can provide a powerful source of healing and rejuvenation.

Nature has long been revered for its ability to soothe the soul and restore balance to the mind and body. From the gentle rustle of leaves in the breeze to the rhythmic lapping of waves against the shore, the sights, sounds, and sensations of the natural world have a profound effect on our senses, evoking feelings of calmness, tranquility, and awe. Research has shown that spending time in nature can reduce stress, lower blood pressure, and boost mood, leading to improved overall health and well-being.

One of the most remarkable aspects of nature's healing power is its ability to induce a state of mindfulness – a state of focused awareness and presence in the present moment. When we immerse ourselves in the sights and sounds of nature, we become attuned to the rhythm of the natural world, grounding us in the here and now and freeing us from the worries and anxieties of everyday life. Whether it's a leisurely stroll through a forest, a quiet moment by a babbling brook, or a breathtaking sunset over the horizon, nature has a way of quieting the mind and nourishing the soul.

Moreover, nature offers a sense of connection and belonging that is often lacking in our increasingly urbanized and technologically-driven world. In nature, we are reminded of our place in the larger web of life, humbled by the vastness and beauty of the natural world. Whether it's the sight of a majestic mountain range, the sound of birdsong in the trees, or the feeling of soft grass beneath our feet, nature invites us to pause, reflect, and reconnect with the essence of our humanity.

Furthermore, nature provides a space for introspection and self-discovery, offering a refuge for contemplation, creativity, and spiritual renewal. In the quiet solitude of the natural world, we can listen to the whispers of our own hearts, gain clarity and perspective on life's challenges, and tap into a deeper sense of meaning and purpose. Whether it's finding inspiration for creative endeavors, seeking solace in times of grief or loss, or simply finding a moment of respite from the demands of everyday life, nature holds the key to unlocking the mysteries of the human spirit.

In summary, the healing power of nature is a timeless and universal phenomenon that has been celebrated by cultures around the world for centuries. From ancient wisdom traditions to modern scientific research, the benefits of spending time in nature are undeniable. Whether it's reducing stress, boosting mood, fostering mindfulness, or nurturing a sense of connection and belonging, nature has the power to heal, inspire, and transform us in profound ways. By rekindling our relationship with the natural world and embracing its beauty and wonder, we can find solace, serenity, and renewal in the embrace of Mother Earth.

Summary: In this chapter, we explored the healing power of nature and its profound impact on our physical, mental, and emotional well-being. From reducing stress and boosting mood to fostering mindfulness and promoting connection, nature offers a wealth of benefits for personal growth and healing. By reconnecting with the natural world and embracing its beauty and wonder, we can find solace, serenity, and renewal in the embrace of Mother Earth.

Chapter 15: Exploring the Wonders of the Great Outdoors

In today's fast-paced world, where technology dominates our lives and urban landscapes sprawl endlessly, the call of the great outdoors beckons with a promise of adventure, discovery, and rejuvenation. In this chapter, we embark on a journey into the heart of nature, exploring the wonders of the great outdoors and uncovering the myriad delights that await us beyond the confines of civilization.

The great outdoors offers a boundless playground for exploration and discovery, with its vast expanses of forests, mountains, rivers, and deserts serving as the backdrop for a myriad of outdoor activities. Whether it's hiking through rugged mountain trails, kayaking down meandering rivers, or camping beneath a canopy of stars, the possibilities for adventure are endless. Each new experience in nature brings with it a sense of wonder and excitement, as we marvel at the beauty and diversity of the natural world.

Moreover, the great outdoors provides a sanctuary for solitude and reflection, offering a respite from the noise and distractions of modern life. In the quiet serenity of nature, we can escape the pressures of work and society, and reconnect with ourselves on a deeper level. Whether it's sitting by a tranquil lake, listening to the symphony of birdsong in the trees, or gazing up at the vast expanse of the night sky, the great outdoors offers a space for contemplation, introspection, and renewal.

Furthermore, exploring the great outdoors fosters a sense of connection and stewardship for the natural world, instilling in us a deep appreciation and respect for the environment. As we immerse ourselves in the beauty and wonder of nature, we come to understand our interconnectedness with all living things, and our responsibility to protect and preserve the planet for future generations. Whether it's picking up litter on a hiking trail, participating in a beach cleanup, or supporting conservation efforts in our local community, each small act of stewardship helps to ensure the health and vitality of our natural world.

In addition, the great outdoors offers a wealth of physical and mental health benefits, with research showing that spending time in nature can improve mood, reduce stress, and boost overall well-being. Whether it's the invigorating rush of adrenaline during a challenging hike, the meditative calm of a yoga session in the park, or the restorative effects of simply breathing in the fresh air, nature has a profound impact on our physical, mental, and emotional health.

In summary, exploring the wonders of the great outdoors is a transformative journey that offers a wealth of benefits for personal growth, health, and well-being. Whether it's embarking on a new adventure, finding solace in the quiet beauty of nature, or fostering a deeper connection with the environment, the great outdoors invites us to step outside of our comfort zones and embrace the wonders of the natural world. By immersing ourselves in nature's beauty and bounty, we can find inspiration, renewal, and a sense of awe that enriches our lives in countless ways.

Summary: In this chapter, we embarked on a journey into the heart of nature, exploring the wonders of the great outdoors and uncovering the myriad delights that await us beyond the confines of civilization. From adventure and discovery to solitude and reflection, the great outdoors offers a wealth of benefits for personal growth, health, and well-being. By immersing ourselves in nature's beauty and bounty, we can find inspiration, renewal, and a sense of awe that enriches our lives in countless ways.

Chapter 16: Capturing Moments of Beauty Through Photography

In today's fast-paced world, where every moment seems to rush past in a blur of activity, photography offers us a powerful tool for slowing down and savoring the beauty that surrounds us. In this chapter, we explore the art of photography as a means of capturing moments of beauty, finding inspiration in the everyday, and cultivating a deeper appreciation for the world around us.

Photography is more than just a hobby or a profession; it is a way of seeing and experiencing the world. Through the lens of a camera, we have the ability to frame moments in time, freeze fleeting emotions, and immortalize memories that might otherwise be lost to the passage of time. Whether it's the soft glow of a sunrise, the delicate dance of a butterfly, or the joyous laughter of a child, photography allows us to preserve these moments of beauty and share them with others.

Moreover, photography encourages us to slow down and pay attention to the world around us. In our fast-paced lives, it's all too easy to overlook the small moments of beauty that surround us each day. But through the practice of photography, we learn to see the world with fresh eyes, noticing the play of light and shadow, the symmetry of nature, and the subtle details that make each moment unique. By taking the time to compose our shots thoughtfully and intentionally, we become more attuned to the beauty that exists all around us.

Furthermore, photography serves as a form of self-expression and creativity, allowing us to tell stories, convey emotions, and share our unique perspective with the world. Whether we're capturing the grandeur of a majestic landscape or the intimacy of a quiet moment between loved ones, photography offers us a means of expressing ourselves and connecting with others on a deeper level. Through our photographs, we can communicate our passions, our values, and our vision for the world, leaving a lasting impression on those who view our work.

In addition, photography has the power to inspire mindfulness and presence in our daily lives. When we're behind the lens of a camera, we're fully engaged in the present moment, focused on capturing the beauty and wonder that surrounds us. Whether we're exploring a new location, experimenting with different techniques, or simply observing the world around us, photography encourages us to be fully present and attentive to the world around us. In this way, photography becomes not just a means of capturing moments of beauty, but a practice of mindfulness and awareness that enriches our lives in countless ways.

In summary, photography is a powerful tool for slowing down, savoring the beauty of the present moment, and cultivating a deeper appreciation for the world around us. By capturing moments of beauty through the lens of a camera, we learn to see the world with fresh eyes, express ourselves creatively, and inspire mindfulness and presence in our daily lives. Through the practice of photography, we can find joy, inspiration, and connection in the simple act of noticing and appreciating the beauty that surrounds us.

Summary: In this chapter, we explored the art of photography as a means of capturing moments of beauty, finding inspiration in the everyday, and cultivating a deeper appreciation for the world around us. Photography encourages us to slow down, pay attention to the world around us, and express ourselves creatively. By capturing moments of beauty through the lens of a camera, we can inspire mindfulness and presence in our daily lives, enriching our experience of the world and fostering a deeper connection to the beauty that surrounds us.

Chapter 17: Embracing Creativity as a Form of Self-Expression

Creativity is a powerful force that resides within each of us, waiting to be unleashed and expressed in myriad ways. In this chapter, we delve into the importance of embracing creativity as a form of self-expression, exploring how it can enrich our lives, foster personal growth, and deepen our connection to ourselves and the world around us.

At its core, creativity is the act of bringing something new and unique into existence, whether it's through art, music, writing, or any other form of expression. It's about tapping into our imagination, intuition, and innermost desires to create something that is a reflection of who we are and what we believe in. By embracing our creative impulses, we open ourselves up to a world of possibilities, where anything is possible and the only limit is our imagination.

Moreover, creativity is a deeply personal and intimate process that allows us to connect with our innermost thoughts, feelings, and experiences. When we engage in creative activities, we're able to express ourselves in ways that words alone cannot capture, tapping into a deeper reservoir of emotion and meaning. Whether it's painting a canvas, composing a song, or writing a poem, creativity gives us a voice and a means of sharing our innermost selves with the world.

Furthermore, creativity is a catalyst for personal growth and self-discovery. When we engage in creative pursuits, we're forced to confront our fears, doubts, and insecurities, pushing past our comfort zones and embracing the unknown. In the process, we learn more about ourselves, our strengths and weaknesses, and what truly matters to us. Creativity challenges us to take risks, experiment with new ideas, and embrace failure as a natural part of the creative process. Through this journey of self-exploration, we come to understand ourselves more deeply and cultivate a greater sense of self-awareness and self-acceptance.

In addition, creativity has the power to inspire and uplift others, fostering connection, empathy, and understanding. When we share our creative work with others, we invite them into our world, offering them a glimpse into our thoughts, feelings, and experiences. In doing so, we create opportunities for connection and dialogue, building bridges across differences and fostering a greater sense of community and belonging. Creativity has the power to transcend boundaries and unite people from all walks of life, reminding us of our shared humanity and the beauty of our collective experience.

In summary, embracing creativity as a form of self-expression is a transformative journey that enriches our lives, fosters personal growth, and deepens our connection to ourselves and the world around us. By tapping into our creative impulses, we're able to express ourselves in ways that are authentic, meaningful, and deeply personal. Creativity challenges us to explore new possibilities, confront our fears, and embrace the unknown, leading to greater self-awareness and self-acceptance. Moreover, creativity has the power to inspire and uplift others, fostering connection, empathy, and understanding. In embracing our creativity, we discover a profound sense of joy, fulfillment, and purpose that enriches every aspect of our lives.

Summary: In this chapter, we explored the importance of embracing creativity as a form of self-expression, highlighting its transformative power to enrich our lives, foster personal growth, and deepen our connection to ourselves and the world around us. Creativity allows us to express ourselves authentically and meaningfully, challenging us to explore new possibilities and embrace the unknown. Moreover, creativity has the power to inspire and uplift others, fostering connection, empathy, and understanding. By embracing our creativity, we embark on a journey of self-discovery and personal fulfillment that enriches every aspect of our lives.

Chapter 18: Building Meaningful Connections in a Digital Age

In today's fast-paced, technology-driven world, it's easier than ever to stay connected with others. Social media, messaging apps, and video calls make it possible to communicate with people from around the globe instantaneously. However, amid the convenience of digital communication, there's a growing concern about the quality of our connections. In this chapter, we explore the importance of building meaningful connections in a digital age, examining how technology impacts our relationships and offering strategies for cultivating deeper, more authentic connections in an increasingly virtual world.

Technology has undoubtedly revolutionized the way we communicate and connect with others. Platforms like Facebook, Instagram, and Twitter allow us to stay updated on the lives of friends and family, while messaging apps like WhatsApp and Slack enable real-time communication regardless of geographical distance. Video conferencing tools like Zoom have become indispensable for remote work and virtual gatherings, bringing people together in ways that were previously unimaginable. In many ways, technology has made it easier than ever to connect with others and maintain relationships across time and space.

However, amid the convenience of digital communication, there's a downside to our increasingly connected world. Studies have shown that excessive use of social media can lead to feelings of loneliness, isolation, and inadequacy. The curated nature of social media feeds can foster unrealistic expectations and comparisons, leading to a sense of disconnection from others. Moreover, the prevalence of digital communication can sometimes detract from the quality of our interactions, leading to shallow, surface-level connections that lack depth and authenticity.

Despite these challenges, it's still possible to build meaningful connections in a digital age. The key lies in being intentional about how we use technology and prioritizing quality over quantity in our relationships. Rather than passively scrolling through social media feeds, we can actively engage with others by reaching out directly, sharing meaningful experiences, and fostering genuine connections. By using technology as a tool to facilitate deeper communication and connection, we can overcome the barriers that often hinder our ability to form authentic relationships in a digital age.

Moreover, building meaningful connections in a digital age requires us to be mindful of the ways in which technology can impact our relationships. While digital communication can be convenient and efficient, it's important to recognize its limitations and make time for face-to-face interactions whenever possible. Whether it's meeting up with friends for coffee, attending social events, or simply spending time together offline, prioritizing real-world interactions can help strengthen our connections and foster a greater sense of intimacy and closeness.

Furthermore, building meaningful connections in a digital age requires us to be vulnerable and authentic in our interactions. Rather than hiding behind a carefully curated online persona, we can strive to be genuine and transparent with others, sharing our thoughts, feelings, and experiences openly and honestly. By being vulnerable with others, we create opportunities for deeper connection and understanding, fostering trust, empathy, and intimacy in our relationships.

In summary, building meaningful connections in a digital age requires us to be intentional, mindful, and authentic in our interactions. While technology has made it easier than ever to stay connected with others, it's important to recognize the limitations of digital communication and make time for face-to-face interactions whenever possible. By prioritizing quality over quantity in our relationships, being vulnerable and authentic with others, and actively engaging in meaningful conversations and experiences, we can cultivate deeper, more fulfilling connections in an increasingly virtual world.

Summary: In this chapter, we explored the importance of building meaningful connections in a digital age, acknowledging the benefits and challenges of technology in our relationships. While technology has made it easier than ever to stay connected with others, it's important to be mindful of its limitations and prioritize quality over quantity in our interactions. By being intentional, authentic, and vulnerable in our relationships, and making time for face-to-face interactions whenever possible, we can cultivate deeper, more fulfilling connections in an increasingly virtual world.

Chapter 19: Nurturing Relationships Through Quality Time

In today's fast-paced world, where our schedules are often packed with work, responsibilities, and various commitments, finding time to nurture our relationships can be challenging. However, amidst the hustle and bustle of daily life, it's essential to prioritize quality time with our loved ones. In this chapter, we explore the importance of nurturing relationships through quality time, examining how meaningful connections are strengthened by shared experiences and offering strategies for carving out time for loved ones despite our busy schedules.

Quality time refers to the intentional, focused attention we dedicate to our relationships, free from distractions and interruptions. It's about being fully present with our loved ones, engaging in meaningful conversations, and sharing experiences that deepen our connection. Whether it's spending an evening together cooking a meal, going for a walk in nature, or simply enjoying each other's company at home, quality time allows us to nurture our relationships and create lasting memories with those we care about.

One of the most significant benefits of quality time is its ability to strengthen bonds and foster a greater sense of connection between individuals. When we dedicate uninterrupted time to our loved ones, we create opportunities for meaningful conversations and shared experiences that deepen our understanding of one another and strengthen our emotional connection. Quality time allows us to express our love and appreciation for one another in meaningful ways, building trust, intimacy, and resilience in our relationships.

Moreover, quality time serves as a buffer against the stresses and pressures of daily life, providing us with a sense of comfort, support, and belonging. In moments of joy, laughter, and shared experiences, we find solace and rejuvenation, reminding us of the importance of our relationships and the value of human connection. Quality time allows us to recharge our emotional batteries, helping us navigate life's challenges with greater resilience and grace.

Despite its importance, finding time for quality time can be challenging in today's fast-paced world. Our busy schedules, work commitments, and various responsibilities often leave little room for leisure and relaxation, let alone quality time with loved ones. However, prioritizing quality time requires us to be intentional and proactive about carving out time for our relationships, even amidst our hectic schedules.

One strategy for prioritizing quality time is to establish regular rituals and traditions that provide opportunities for shared experiences and meaningful connections. Whether it's a weekly family dinner, a monthly movie night, or an annual vacation, establishing rituals and traditions allows us to create dedicated time for our relationships and strengthen bonds with our loved ones. By making quality time a priority in our lives, we demonstrate our commitment to nurturing our relationships and creating lasting memories with those we care about.

Additionally, it's essential to be mindful of how we use our time and to eliminate distractions that detract from our ability to be fully present with our loved ones. Whether it's putting away our phones during dinner, turning off the television during quality time, or setting boundaries with work and other commitments, eliminating distractions allows us to focus on the people and experiences that matter most to us. By being fully present and engaged in our interactions, we create opportunities for deeper connection and intimacy with our loved ones.

In summary, nurturing relationships through quality time is essential for fostering deeper connections, building trust, and creating lasting memories with our loved ones. Despite the challenges of today's fast-paced world, it's crucial to prioritize quality time in our lives and to be intentional about carving out time for our relationships. By establishing rituals and traditions, eliminating distractions, and being fully present in our interactions, we can cultivate meaningful connections and strengthen bonds with those we care about, enriching our lives and bringing us closer together.

Summary: In this chapter, we explored the importance of nurturing relationships through quality time, highlighting its ability to strengthen bonds, foster connection, and create lasting memories with our loved ones. Despite the challenges of today's fast-paced world, it's essential to prioritize quality time in our lives and to be intentional about carving out time for our relationships. By establishing rituals and traditions, eliminating distractions, and being fully present in our interactions, we can cultivate meaningful connections and enrich our lives through shared experiences with those we care about.

Chapter 20: The Art of Simple Pleasures

In a world filled with distractions and complexities, the pursuit of happiness often seems elusive. We find ourselves chasing after material possessions, success, and status, believing that these external factors will bring us fulfillment. However, amidst the noise and chaos of modern life, we often overlook the simple pleasures that can bring us true joy and contentment. In this chapter, we explore the art of simple pleasures, examining how embracing life's small joys can lead to greater happiness and satisfaction.

The art of simple pleasures lies in finding joy and satisfaction in life's everyday moments, regardless of how mundane or ordinary they may seem. It's about cultivating a sense of gratitude and appreciation for the small things in life, from savoring a cup of coffee in the morning to watching the sunset in the evening. By shifting our focus away from material possessions and external achievements, we can find happiness in the present moment and cultivate a greater sense of contentment in our lives.

One of the key elements of the art of simple pleasures is mindfulness – the practice of being fully present and aware of our experiences without judgment. When we approach life with a mindful attitude, we become more attuned to the beauty and wonder that surrounds us, allowing us to fully appreciate the simple pleasures that enrich our lives. Whether it's feeling the warmth of the sun on our skin or listening to the sound of birds chirping outside our window, mindfulness helps us connect with the present moment and find joy in the here and now.

Moreover, the art of simple pleasures encourages us to slow down and savor life's moments, rather than rushing through them in pursuit of the next big thing. In a society that glorifies busyness and productivity, we often overlook the importance of taking time to rest, relax, and recharge. By embracing simple pleasures, we can create moments of peace and tranquility in our lives, allowing us to escape the stresses and pressures of daily life and find solace in the present moment.

Simple pleasures can take many forms, from spending time with loved ones to engaging in creative pursuits or immersing ourselves in nature. Whether it's going for a walk in the park, reading a good book, or enjoying a home-cooked meal, these small acts of self-care can bring us immense joy and satisfaction. By incorporating simple pleasures into our daily routines, we can cultivate a greater sense of happiness and well-being in our lives, regardless of our circumstances or external factors.

In summary, the art of simple pleasures is about finding joy and contentment in life's everyday moments, regardless of how small or insignificant they may seem. By cultivating a mindful attitude and slowing down to savor life's moments, we can connect with the present moment and find happiness in the here and now. Whether it's enjoying a quiet moment alone or spending time with loved ones, embracing simple pleasures can enrich our lives and bring us greater fulfillment and satisfaction.

Chapter 21: Letting Nature Guide Your Journey

In the fast-paced, technology-driven world we live in, it's easy to feel disconnected from nature. Many of us spend our days indoors, surrounded by concrete buildings and artificial lights, rarely taking the time to appreciate the natural world around us. However, nature has a way of guiding us on our journey and providing us with the wisdom and inspiration we need to navigate life's challenges. In this chapter, we explore the profound impact that nature can have on our lives and how we can let it guide our journey towards greater fulfillment and inner peace.

Nature has a way of captivating our senses and stirring our souls in ways that nothing else can. From the gentle rustle of leaves in the wind to the soothing sound of water flowing in a stream, nature has a way of calming our minds and rejuvenating our spirits. When we immerse ourselves in the natural world, we are reminded of the interconnectedness of all living things and our place within the larger ecosystem of life.

Moreover, nature has a way of teaching us valuable lessons about resilience, adaptability, and the cycle of life and death. In nature, we witness the beauty of growth and renewal, as plants emerge from the soil, flowers bloom, and trees shed their leaves in preparation for the changing seasons. We also learn to embrace change and uncertainty, as nature is constantly evolving and adapting to new circumstances and challenges.

One of the most profound ways that nature can guide our journey is by helping us reconnect with our inner selves and tap into our intuition and inner wisdom. When we spend time in nature, away from the distractions and noise of modern life, we are better able to listen to the whispers of our hearts and the guidance of our intuition. Nature has a way of quieting the mind and opening the heart, allowing us to access deeper truths and insights about ourselves and our purpose in life.

Furthermore, nature has a way of healing us on a physical, emotional, and spiritual level. Studies have shown that spending time in nature can reduce stress, anxiety, and depression, improve mood and cognitive function, and boost overall well-being. Whether it's taking a leisurely stroll through the woods, practicing yoga in a peaceful meadow, or simply sitting quietly by a lake, nature has a way of restoring balance and harmony to our lives.

In summary, nature has a profound impact on our lives and has the power to guide us on our journey towards greater fulfillment and inner peace. By immersing ourselves in the natural world and reconnecting with the rhythms of the earth, we can tap into our intuition, find inspiration and wisdom, and experience healing on a deep level. Whether it's taking a walk in the park, spending time in a garden, or exploring a remote wilderness area, let nature be your guide as you navigate the ups and downs of life's journey.

Chapter 22: Embracing Imperfection and Finding Peace

In a world that often values perfection and flawlessness, the idea of embracing imperfection may seem counterintuitive. However, learning to accept and even celebrate our imperfections can lead to a greater sense of peace, self-acceptance, and overall well-being. In this chapter, we delve into the importance of embracing imperfection and the profound impact it can have on our lives.

Imperfection is a fundamental aspect of the human experience. No one is perfect, and striving for perfection only leads to frustration, stress, and unhappiness. When we embrace our imperfections, we free ourselves from the unrealistic expectations and standards that society often imposes upon us. Instead of focusing on our flaws and shortcomings, we can learn to appreciate our unique strengths, talents, and qualities that make us who we are.

Moreover, embracing imperfection allows us to cultivate greater compassion and empathy towards ourselves and others. When we accept our own imperfections, we are better able to extend grace and understanding to those around us who may also be struggling with their own insecurities and challenges. Rather than judging ourselves and others harshly for our perceived shortcomings, we can offer kindness, support, and encouragement as we navigate life's ups and downs together.

Embracing imperfection also frees us from the fear of failure and the need for external validation. When we let go of the pressure to be perfect, we can take risks, try new things, and pursue our passions without fear of judgment or criticism. We come to realize that failure is not something to be ashamed of, but rather an opportunity for growth, learning, and self-discovery. By embracing imperfection, we can live more authentically and courageously, trusting in our own abilities and intuition to guide us on our journey.

Furthermore, embracing imperfection allows us to cultivate a greater sense of gratitude and appreciation for the beauty and richness of life. When we let go of the need to control every outcome and circumstance, we can open ourselves up to the unexpected joys, surprises, and blessings that come our way. We learn to find beauty in the imperfect moments, the messy experiences, and the unexpected detours that life throws our way.

In summary, embracing imperfection is a powerful practice that can lead to greater peace, happiness, and fulfillment in life. By letting go of the pressure to be perfect and accepting ourselves as we are, flaws and all, we can cultivate greater self-compassion, empathy, and resilience. Embracing imperfection allows us to live more authentically, courageously, and joyfully, embracing the beauty of life's imperfect moments and finding peace in the midst of chaos.

Chapter 23: Embracing Imperfection and Finding Peace

In a world that often esteems perfection as the ultimate goal, embracing imperfection may seem contradictory. However, acknowledging and embracing our imperfections can lead to profound inner peace, self-acceptance, and overall well-being. This chapter explores the significance of embracing imperfection and its transformative effects on our lives.

Imperfection is an inherent part of the human condition. No individual is flawless, and the pursuit of perfection often results in frustration, stress, and discontentment. When we embrace our imperfections, we liberate ourselves from the unrealistic standards imposed by society. Rather than fixating on our flaws and limitations, we learn to recognize and appreciate our unique strengths, talents, and attributes that shape our identity.

Furthermore, embracing imperfection fosters compassion and empathy, both towards ourselves and others. By accepting our own flaws and vulnerabilities, we become more understanding and forgiving of the imperfections in those around us. Rather than harshly judging ourselves and others, we extend kindness, empathy, and support as we navigate life's challenges together.

Embracing imperfection also liberates us from the fear of failure and the need for external validation. When we release the pressure to attain perfection, we can take risks, explore new opportunities, and pursue our passions without the fear of judgment or criticism. Failure ceases to be a source of shame, but rather becomes a stepping stone towards growth, resilience, and self-discovery.

Moreover, embracing imperfection cultivates a profound sense of gratitude and appreciation for life's complexities and nuances. By relinquishing the desire to control every aspect of our lives, we become receptive to the unexpected joys, serendipitous moments, and unanticipated blessings that unfold before us. We learn to find beauty in life's imperfections, embracing the messy, unpredictable aspects of existence with open arms.

In essence, embracing imperfection is a liberating practice that can bring about profound peace, contentment, and fulfillment. By embracing our imperfections and accepting ourselves unconditionally, we foster greater self-compassion, resilience, and authenticity. Embracing imperfection empowers us to live courageously, authentically, and wholeheartedly, finding solace and tranquility amidst life's uncertainties and complexities.

Summary: Embracing imperfection is a transformative practice that leads to inner peace, self-acceptance, and fulfillment. By acknowledging and embracing our flaws, we free ourselves from the burden of unrealistic expectations and societal pressures. Embracing imperfection fosters compassion, empathy, and resilience, enabling us to navigate life's challenges with grace and courage. Moreover, embracing imperfection allows us to cultivate gratitude and appreciation for the beauty of life's imperfections, finding peace and contentment in the midst of life's uncertainties. Ultimately, embracing imperfection empowers us to live authentically and wholeheartedly, embracing the full spectrum of human experience with openness and acceptance.

Chapter 24: Living Authentically: Honoring Your True Self

Living authentically is about embracing your true self and aligning your actions, beliefs, and values with who you genuinely are. In a world filled with societal expectations and pressures to conform, living authentically requires courage, self-awareness, and a willingness to embrace your uniqueness. This chapter delves into the importance of living authentically and the transformative impact it can have on your life.

Authentic living begins with self-awareness and introspection. It involves a deep exploration of your values, passions, and beliefs, as well as an honest examination of your strengths, weaknesses, and desires. By gaining clarity about who you are at your core, you can make choices and decisions that are in alignment with your authentic self, rather than succumbing to external influences or societal expectations.

Living authentically also entails embracing vulnerability and embracing your imperfections. It requires the courage to show up as your true self, even when it feels uncomfortable or challenging. By allowing yourself to be vulnerable and authentic, you create deeper connections with others and foster genuine relationships built on trust, empathy, and mutual respect.

Moreover, living authentically empowers you to pursue your passions and dreams wholeheartedly. When you honor your true self and follow your inner guidance, you unleash your full potential and tap into a source of creativity, inspiration, and fulfillment. Authentic living is about expressing your unique talents and gifts authentically, without fear of judgment or rejection.

Furthermore, living authentically requires setting boundaries and prioritizing self-care. It involves honoring your needs, values, and well-being, even if it means saying no to others or making unpopular decisions. By prioritizing self-care and setting boundaries, you protect your energy and preserve your authenticity in the face of external pressures and expectations.

Living authentically also involves embracing change and embracing the journey of self-discovery and growth. It requires a willingness to step outside your comfort zone, take risks, and embrace new opportunities for personal and spiritual development. By embracing change and growth, you open yourself up to new possibilities and experiences that enrich your life and expand your horizons.

In essence, living authentically is a journey of self-discovery, self-expression, and self-empowerment. It requires courage, vulnerability, and a willingness to embrace your uniqueness fully. By honoring your true self and living in alignment with your values and passions, you cultivate a sense of purpose, fulfillment, and inner peace that transcends external circumstances.

Summary: Living authentically is about embracing your true self and aligning your actions, beliefs, and values with who you genuinely are. It requires self-awareness, vulnerability, and a willingness to embrace your uniqueness fully. By honoring your true self and living in alignment with your values and passions, you cultivate a sense of purpose, fulfillment, and inner peace that transcends external circumstances. Living authentically empowers you to pursue your passions, set boundaries, and prioritize self-care, allowing you to live a life that is true to who you are at your core.

Chapter 25: Cultivating Gratitude and Appreciation

In a world filled with distractions and challenges, cultivating gratitude and appreciation is a powerful practice that can transform our perspective and bring more joy, fulfillment, and peace into our lives. This chapter explores the importance of gratitude and appreciation and offers practical strategies for incorporating them into our daily lives.

Gratitude is the practice of recognizing and acknowledging the blessings, gifts, and positive aspects of our lives, both big and small. It involves cultivating an attitude of thankfulness and appreciation for the people, experiences, and opportunities that enrich our lives. By focusing on what we have rather than what we lack, gratitude allows us to shift our perspective and cultivate a sense of abundance and contentment.

Appreciation goes hand in hand with gratitude and involves recognizing the value, beauty, and significance of the people and things around us. It entails taking the time to notice and savor the simple pleasures, moments of beauty, and acts of kindness that enhance our daily lives. By cultivating appreciation, we deepen our connection to the world around us and foster a greater sense of joy and fulfillment.

Practicing gratitude and appreciation offers a myriad of benefits for our mental, emotional, and physical well-being. Research has shown that gratitude practices can improve mood, reduce stress, enhance resilience, and strengthen relationships. By focusing on the positive aspects of our lives, we train our brains to become more attuned to joy, love, and abundance, leading to greater overall happiness and life satisfaction.

There are many simple yet effective ways to cultivate gratitude and appreciation in our daily lives. One powerful practice is keeping a gratitude journal, where we write down three things we're thankful for each day. This practice helps us become more mindful of the blessings in our lives and reinforces a positive outlook. Additionally, expressing gratitude verbally or through acts of kindness can strengthen our relationships and foster a sense of connection and belonging.

Mindfulness meditation is another powerful tool for cultivating gratitude and appreciation. By bringing our awareness to the present moment and focusing on our breath, sensations, or surroundings, we can cultivate a sense of presence and appreciation for the beauty and wonder of life. Incorporating mindfulness into our daily routines can help us become more attuned to the richness of each moment and develop a deeper sense of gratitude.

Spending time in nature is another powerful way to cultivate gratitude and appreciation. By immersing ourselves in the beauty of the natural world, we can gain a greater appreciation for the interconnectedness of all living things and develop a sense of awe and reverence for the Earth. Whether it's taking a walk in the park, watching a sunset, or listening to birdsong, nature has a way of nourishing our souls and reminding us of the beauty and abundance that surrounds us.

In summary, cultivating gratitude and appreciation is a transformative practice that can bring more joy, fulfillment, and peace into our lives. By focusing on the positive aspects of our lives and cultivating an attitude of thankfulness and appreciation, we can shift our perspective and foster a greater sense of abundance and contentment. Whether through journaling, mindfulness meditation, or spending time in nature, there are many simple yet powerful ways to incorporate gratitude and appreciation into our daily lives and experience the profound benefits they offer.

Chapter 26: The Journey of Self-Discovery

Introduction: The journey of self-discovery is a profound and transformative process that involves exploring the depths of our inner being to uncover our true essence, values, and purpose in life. In this chapter, we will delve into the importance of embarking on this journey, the challenges and rewards it entails, and practical strategies for deepening our self-awareness and understanding.

Exploring the Inner Landscape: Self-discovery begins with turning our attention inward and exploring the vast and intricate landscape of our inner world. It involves becoming curious and open to understanding our thoughts, emotions, beliefs, and patterns of behavior. By cultivating self-awareness, we can gain insights into our motivations, desires, and fears, and uncover the underlying factors that shape our perceptions and actions.

Embracing Vulnerability: A key aspect of the journey of self-discovery is embracing vulnerability and allowing ourselves to be authentic and vulnerable with ourselves and others. It involves facing our fears, insecurities, and uncertainties with courage and compassion, and embracing the full spectrum of our emotions and experiences. By embracing vulnerability, we can cultivate deeper connections with ourselves and others, and foster a greater sense of authenticity and wholeness.

Navigating Inner Resistance: As we embark on the journey of self-discovery, we may encounter inner resistance in the form of self-doubt, fear, and limiting beliefs. These inner barriers can hold us back from fully embracing our true selves and realizing our potential. By acknowledging and gently exploring our inner resistance, we can begin to dismantle the barriers that stand in the way of our growth and transformation.

Cultivating Self-Compassion: Self-discovery is a journey of self-compassion and self-acceptance, where we learn to treat ourselves with kindness, understanding, and empathy. It involves recognizing and embracing our imperfections and vulnerabilities, and extending the same compassion and forgiveness to ourselves that we would offer to a dear friend. By cultivating self-compassion, we can heal past wounds, release self-judgment, and foster a deep sense of love and acceptance for ourselves.

Honoring Your Authentic Self: At the heart of the journey of self-discovery is the quest to honor and embody our authentic selves. It involves aligning with our core values, passions, and inner wisdom, and living in alignment with our true purpose and calling. By honoring our authentic selves, we can experience greater fulfillment, joy, and meaning in our lives, and contribute our unique gifts and talents to the world.

Summary: The journey of self-discovery is a transformative process that involves exploring the depths of our inner being to uncover our true essence, values, and purpose in life. It begins with turning our attention inward and exploring the vast landscape of our inner world with curiosity and openness. Along the way, we may encounter inner resistance, self-doubt, and limiting beliefs, but by embracing vulnerability, cultivating self-compassion, and honoring our authentic selves, we can navigate these challenges and embark on a path of deep healing and transformation. Ultimately, the journey of self-discovery is a journey of self-acceptance, self-love, and self-empowerment, where we learn to embrace the fullness of who we are and live authentically and wholeheartedly in alignment with our true selves.

Conclusion - Embracing Serenity in a Chaotic World

In this final chapter, we reflect on the journey we've taken together to explore the art of slowing down and discovering life's beauty. Throughout this book, we've delved into various aspects of embracing serenity amidst the chaos of modern life. As we conclude our exploration, we revisit the key themes and lessons learned, and discuss how we can continue to cultivate a sense of peace and tranquility in our everyday lives.

Reflecting on the Journey: Our journey began with an acknowledgment of the frantic pace of modern life and the need to pause, reflect, and reconnect with ourselves and the world around us. We explored the challenges of decision paralysis, the allure of productivity obsession, and the importance of embracing imperfection and finding peace in the midst of chaos. Along the way, we discovered the healing power of nature, the joy of leisure and hobbies, and the beauty of living authentically and honoring our true selves.

Embracing Serenity: As we reflect on our journey, we recognize that embracing serenity is not about escaping from the chaos of the world, but rather, finding inner peace and tranquility amidst it. It involves cultivating mindfulness, gratitude, and compassion in our daily lives, and learning to let go of the need for constant busyness and achievement. By slowing down and savoring the present moment, we can experience a deeper sense of connection, purpose, and fulfillment.

Practical Strategies for Cultivating Serenity: To continue our journey towards serenity, we can incorporate practical strategies into our daily routines. These may include mindfulness meditation, journaling, spending time in nature, practicing self-care, and nurturing meaningful connections with others. By prioritizing our well-being and making conscious choices that align with our values and priorities, we can create a life filled with serenity, joy, and meaning.

Embracing the Journey: As we conclude our exploration, we recognize that the journey towards serenity is ongoing and ever-evolving. It requires patience, courage, and commitment to continue exploring and embracing the beauty of life amidst its challenges and uncertainties. By remaining open to growth, learning, and transformation, we can continue to cultivate serenity and live more fully in alignment with our true selves.

Summary: In conclusion, the journey of embracing serenity in a chaotic world is a deeply transformative and rewarding process. It involves slowing down, reconnecting with ourselves and the world around us, and cultivating a sense of peace and tranquility amidst the hustle and bustle of modern life. By reflecting on our experiences, learning from our challenges, and embracing the beauty of life's imperfections, we can continue to journey towards serenity with courage, grace, and resilience. As we navigate the complexities of life, may we remember to pause, breathe, and embrace the serenity that lies within us, always.

Printed in Great Britain
by Amazon